No Hogwash

Pray
and
Grow Rich

Pray and Grow Rich
By: Michael Von Irvin, MBA, BSN, RN

It is not the strongest of the species that survives, not the most intelligent that survives. It is the one that is the most adaptable to change.
—Charles Darwin

Testimonials
For Michael Von Irvin

Michael
"My pleasure to add a distinguished professional, such as yourself, to my circle of friends. All the best to you and your loved ones."
Father of Steve Job's Founder Of Apple Computers
John Jandali

Author • "America's #1 Marketing Wizard"
•
• "The Deal Maker" • "Master Negotiator" A lot of people are saying great things about Mike Von Irvin.

Former New York City Healthcare executive. Former VP of AlphaCare and Director of Marketing for MLTC Consulting. Serial Entrepreneur.

Past appearances with Geraldo Rivera, Thomas Mesereau (Michael Jackson's Attorney), Tracy Morgan, Prince Royce, Rafael Furcal and many other celebrities, politicians, and sports stars.

BRANDING–My friend marketing whiz Michael Von Irvin says branding is pointless without good Copywriting to
back it up. I think he's right.
—David Garfinkel (copywriting legend)

John Fleck
Owner
Wanted to give a shout out to Michael Von Irvin. In one day his coaching and guidance has made a huge difference in the direction of my business.

—Brad Szollose with Michael Von Irvin. My second business meeting in the city was with businessman, speaker and trainer Michael Von Irvin and his wife Bella.

Some of my clients have included large healthcare plans such as AlphaCare NY - now Magellan Health. Fitango - innovative patient engagement solutions help to reduce costly readmissions and improve outcomes - NY, Special Touch Homecare LHCSA NY, ASDC, MD's, Nurse Practitioner Groups, FESCO Fire Equipment Company Birmingham/Atlanta/International, Irvin Brother's World Imports, IFPA - International Fire Protection Academy, Hood Master, Southern Fire Solutions,

NAFFCO - Dubai, Exit Logic, Jessup Mfg - Chicago, MeridianRx (PBM) - Detroit, and other Healthcare Plans, Providers, Clarity, Tyco, SimplexGrinnell, FireMaster, Clinical, IT, Businesses, Marketing Related Companies, US Military Iraq.

Introduction To
No Hogwash Books

This book is not meant to be a masterpiece of grammar. There may be grammatical mistakes. In the spirit of No Hogwash Books, we just try to get straight to the point and to hammer these
points home. We are honored that you chose this book to read and study. Some topics in this book may be covered repetitively intentionally.

REMEMBER: It is what you get out of a book that is important. This book is not meant to cover all portions of the subject. It is meant to help you. In order to learn more and grow more we also have courses designed for each subject of interest.

Thanks so much. We are very grateful to consider you a friend.

For more info visit
www.michaelvonirvin.com Or
www.nohogwashbooks.com

If you are going to make a real change for the better, it will not be easy at first.   And know this.....there are a lot of people who are looking out for your best interest. However, there are also a lot of people who will try to control you. Many years ago, I had to break free of negative people and learn how to live my life to the fullest.

- *Michael Von Irvin*

No Hogwash
Pray
and
Grow Rich

TESTIMONY:

Michael's short book on sales techniques gets right to the point. It showcases Jesus as the greatest salesman in history.

His pitch is not the idea of Jesus being a manipulative sort of salesman. Not at all! It shows that Jesus thoroughly understood the concepts of persuasion behind all good sales techniques.

Michael covers all the important persuasive sales techniques and shows how Jesus was a master of these techniques. Techniques like: the power of value, building a following, using word of mouth, and using your passion and much more. This short book has an interesting concept and can be easily digested in a single sitting.

- Steve Scott
Author of "How to Write a Nonfiction eBook in 21 Days" and many more books.

Steve Scott is a famous, world-renowned author.

Leverage The Powers of Prayer To Grow Rich

Michael Von Irvin
MBA

www.michaelvonirvin.com

How to Achieve or Receive Anything Good Through The Power of Prayer

By Michael Von Irvin

Is Any Religion Real?

Often there is an argument about whether one religion is real or true while another is false. That decision can only be made by the believer of the particular religion. Did Christ really die on the cross? Did he really say exactly the words that the New Testament declares? Who knows? One should not care. When you drink water do you look down into the glass and see the water molecules? Do you argue over their arrangement? Do you say that one is out of alignment with another molecule? No. Yet, the water quenches your thirst, cools your body, fills your cells and energies your life. You then carry that water to another area of the universe when you walk away from the source. That water becomes something different inside of you. If fuels you. It allows you to create, think, do, and to multiply your expression of faith that the water was okay to drink. Faith in religion, almost any religion, can do the same thing. Faith in the water is not faith in how the water came to be. It is only faith and that faith, just like the water, doesn't have to be broken down and examined to be consumed and to be powerful.

Faith, thus, is a multiplier. It magnifies that which we have at our disposal. We cannot seek to know everything about nothing or everything about everything. It would be better to seek to know nothing about everything than everything about nothing. We, who have faith, actually know more than everything about everything. With faith, everything becomes more than we could ever imagine it could become. We would never have the time in a lifetime to examine what one drop of water will become in infinite time. Our faith supersedes the need to know this. Faith is like an atom bomb being created from one drop of water. You may call this blind faith. Would you still drink a glass of water if you were thirsty and blindfolded? Of course you would. Faith is usually only blind when we over examine its origin and meaning. Faith is a trillion times more powerful than its meaning. So, seeking its meaning is like trying to examine air inside the tire of a car instead of driving with your family on an enjoyable vacation.

Where does milk come from? Most people will say, "From a cow, of course." But in fact, milk comes from grass and water. Cows eat grass and drink water and produce milk. Milk then becomes cheese and yogurt. Milk, cheese and yogurt become energy within people. People do miraculous things with the energy derived from grass and water. And even so, the grass and water come from somewhere. We need not observe where they come from to reap the benefits of a doctor saving a patient's life with the energy received from eating food.

We can conclude that religion is real. Faith is powerful.

But how do we develop power and energy through faith?

In the next segment, I will tell you how you can take faith which is already one of the most powerful concepts in the universe and make it exponentially more powerful through a very simple technique that is commonly misunderstood and overlooked.

Prayer, the multiplier of the Power of Faith

To examine and explain the power of prayer as a multiplier of the power of faith, I'm going to use a story. The story, though fictional, is probably as true as any truth ever told. You might ask how a story can be both fictional and true at the same time. To this, I respond, any story can be both fictional and true at the same time if you have faith that the concepts explained within the story explain fundamental and universal truths. Some would say essential, truths.

The Story:

It was a regular day for Tom. He got up early and headed off to work. He adjusted the volume on his radio. He turned on his windshield wipers because it was raining lightly outside. He was half asleep having stayed up late to watch the football game the night before. He was happy because his team won the game. However, he was more worried about the upcoming meeting that he had scheduled with his boss than about the score of the football game.

Suddenly, a deer leaped in front of his car and crashed through the windshield. An antler was sticking through his collar bone. He was bleeding profusely. Luckily he had pulled off to the side of the road. But it was so early in the morning that nobody would likely come to his rescue anytime soon. He removed his seatbelt and leveraged the antler out of his collar bone. He then got out of the car.

After placing pressure on the blood gushing out of his body, he instinctively, got down on his knees and prayed for God to help him. He really had no other choice. He didn't have the energy to search for his cell phone. He was sure that he couldn't even get to his feet again.

Tom was no religious man. In fact, he was agnostic. He had abandoned his religion as a teenager. But he did notice that he had a tendency to automatically pray, a little at least, when he was under a lot of stress or when things seemed hopeless. Just right now, things seemed hopeless. But he didn't really consider that. He only knew that he was dying. He tried to think of his loved ones, but he didn't have the energy to concentrate on them.

At first, he said out loud, "God help me, Man, I'm dying." But then, it became, "God help me, God help me, God please.... ...help me." He could feel himself fading off. He then began to say, "Just give me the strength to stand up one more time. I want to stand up. Stand up. Stand up." As he said this he slowly came to his feet. He then began to walk to the road. He then walked down the road, one slow step after another while saying, "Just one more step, just one more step, just one more step." Soon he reached a service station about a mile and half down the road. From there he went to the hospital by ambulance, received blood transfusions and medical treatment and is alive and well and healthy today. However, he couldn't remember walking to the service station. He only remembers hearing someone saying, "Just one more step, just one more step, just one more step" over and over again.

Did some form of God physically save Tom's life? Did some form of God descend from some form of heaven and lift Tom up and carry him? Does it matter? The real answer lies in the example of looking for water molecules instead of drinking the water when you are thirsty. Only through faith was Tom's life saved. Had he not had at least a little faith in the power of prayer, he would've never gained the strength to stand. Had he not stood up, he would've never walked. And had he not began to walk, he would've never made it to safety.

Prayer is both a catalyst for Faith and a multiplier for Faith. If Faith has more power than an atomic bomb then prayer has the power of a trillion atomic bombs because through prayer we exhibit our faith. We expose our true trust in faith when we pray. We not only ignite the fuse, we create a chain reaction of faith.

Prayer creates a positive energy field around the person who prays. It draws energy from unknown and unexplainable sources. Maybe the energy that is brought about by faith is already within us like an atom that can be split multiple times. Maybe, it comes from up high. Maybe it comes from the far reaches of the universe. It doesn't matter where it comes from. It exists. It's powerful. It can be initiated through prayer and it can be multiplied through prayer. What more do we need to know? Do we need to know the alignment of the water molecules in the water in order to quench our thirst?

How to pray

Praying is simple. If you are confused about how to pray, try this. Sit down with a pen and paper and write, "This is a prayer about what I want." Then continue to list the thing that you want. Don't worry about the fact that some people will tell you that you need to drop to your knees and pray in silence. Or that you need to chant a certain chant.

In saying the above, I'm in no way saying that those religions are not legitimate. But if you are reading this, it is for a specific reason. Something brought you here. You want my help. So, I feel led to give you my help. In doing so, I must give you my help based upon my own beliefs and experience about how prayer has worked in my life.

So, simply make a list of all the things that you want. Think of the universe as a big huge warehouse of good things and great events that can occur. You have to make out a request for these things. It is sort of like ordering off of the internet. You have to make a request before the order can be filled and the item arrives.

However, wish for no evil lest you expose yourself to evil. You are to only list positive things and events that you want to occur. There are three reasons for this. One, even if you were able to bring about bad things, you would regret it. Secondly, you are not likely to create the positive energy necessary to receive great things if you inject evil or negativity into your life. Thirdly, the universal currency of prayer is love. Hate is not accepted here.

Let's get back to our prayer.

People will tell you that it is not okay to ask for personal things or events for yourself. That is their opinion. My opinion, faith, and experiences are different from that. I believe that it is not only okay for you to ask for personal things and occurrences for yourself and your loved ones, (Note your loved ones can include anyone including the whole universe) it is your obligation to the universe.

If you don't ask, don't expect to receive.

God, the universe, whatever you choose to call it, is not as responsive to those who remain silent as to those who express what they want. When I say remain silent, I'm not talking about a particular form of speaking or communication. What I'm referring to is absolute silence or even more confusing, uncertainty. And while I say that I'm not talking about a particular form of communication, it has been my experience that there are methods to exponentially increase your ROP (Return on Prayer).

It is better to silently prayer in your mind than to not pray at all. At least this creates a starting point for letting the universe know what you desire. However, if silent prayer is the starting point, then taking massive action is perhaps the ultimate prayer.

Let me explain, you can sit silently and pray. That will create a certain amount of positive energy and if you have faith you will probably at least take some action toward receiving what you pray for and/or through the miracles of prayer you may receive some or all of what you desire at some point in the future. When and if that will occur, nobody knows.

But if will write out your prayer, explicitly write out what you desire in as much detail as possible without getting carried away about the details, it has been my experience that you will probably receive what you desire. However, you can take this even a step further.

Write out what you desire in your prayer notebook. Then write out a date for when you want to achieve what you desire. Now, you have taken this prayer to a new level. But you can do more.

Write out what you desire, write a date for receiving what you desire, then write what you plan to do to get what you desire. This is last step is commonly referred to as applied faith.

You may say that this sounds a lot like goal setting. That is correct, it is a lot like goal setting, but in goal setting there is no spiritual aspect involved. It is the spiritual aspect, and the knowing that faith, prayer, and spirituality creates an unstoppable energy that will take you beyond simple goal setting to unstoppable achievement.

I still haven't gone through a step by step example of how to write out these unstoppable prayers. I also haven't talked about uncertainty or mixed signals and prayer. Well, maybe next time.

Until then, if I you need to reach me, you can do so
at help@writersprofitguide.com

All the best,

Michael Von Irvin

www.michaelvonirvin.com

Many years ago I read a great book written in English, "The Greatest Salesman in the World" by Og Mandino

A few months ago, I purchased the same book written in Spanish from a street vender in the Dominican Republic. It must have been sitting in his stack of books for many years as it was tattered, torn, and stained from front cover to back. Each page had stains where the book had gotten wet from rain then dried again.

I found myself sitting, drinking coffee and reading this fascinating book while contemplating what if Jesus were a salesman, what would he have done differently? I have concluded that he probably wouldn't have changed a thing. His techniques were perfect for any salesman and every salesman should know these techniques.

My Story:

The title of this has a several meanings first Prayer is important, but working, thinking, and believing are equally important.

Jesus was a salesman in a way. He was not a manipulator, but like all good salespeople he was a great persuader.

The other meaning of the title is that of the story of Jesus. The story of Jesus has survived for thousands of years. It has been sold from one person to the next through the sales techniques that you will learn in this book.

Also, keep in mind that Jesus was a carpenter by trade and not a
"real" salesman. But as it turned out he also was a great salesman.

How can I teach you to sell in the style of Jesus with great results? First of all we are extracting the techniques that came naturally to the greatest salesman who ever existed. Secondly, we are selling in a

(I have packed my Free Newsletters, chalk full of interesting information on business and wealth growth to help keep my subscribers current. You can only get this by signing up

much larger society with very different rules and larger economies than the times Jesus.

Lastly, we don't have the threat of being tortured and put to death for selling.

When I decided to write this book I did so reluctantly. I truly enjoy writing and I enjoy selling, but I never thought that I would be writing a book about how Jesus Christ, who was the greatest salesman to ever exist and very effectively "sold and marketed" his message.

I believe that you must pray for what you want. Why? Praying not only proves your faith, it also increases your faith. You must work also, but if you do the other three things Pray, Think, and Believe, I believe that you will grow richer and wealthy in all parts of your life. This is not only true in regards to money. And I believe you will not need to work as hard. If you do work hard, you will enjoy it infinitely more than if you didn't include the other three elements.

About Me:

I am a son of a preacher, minister, and tent and radio evangelist. My dad supplemented our family's income by selling shoes door to door.

I have spent thousands of hours from the time of my birth listening to stories from both the New Testament and the Old Testament.

Countless people would come to my house for private, one on one, and family counseling with my dad.

As well, I have spent my whole life learning how to sell better and better without using manipulation.

I prefer persuasion to manipulation. There is a subtle difference between the two.

But, after all that, I didn't write this book by choice. I was led to write it.

*Please also let me know if you think of things to add to this book.

Now let's get started.

AnOriginStory

No matter what your religious faith is, you have more than likely heard that Jesus was born from to a virgin named Mary. Mary was married to Joseph.

Joseph knew that Jesus was not just any other child because the angels came to him and told him so.

Joseph took Jesus and Mary on a trip to Bethlehem. There Jesus was born in a manger surrounded by animals.

There was a King named Herod who wanted to kill Jesus because three wise men had informed Herod of the birth of Jesus and that Jesus was the King.

Take away – The importance of an Origin Story is often overlooked, but is one of the most important parts of selling. People and businesses need an origin story.

In fact, almost every super hero has a well-known, easy to follow, easy to repeat, origin story.

Take the time to write out and rehearse your origin story. The most interesting people in the world have one and can tell it with ease.

In fact, many people have several true origin stories.

AStrongHook

"The King is Born"

Could there be a stronger headline or hook than this? It sure got King Herod's attention. After all, he thought he was the King.

Herod so urgently wanted to eliminate this newly born King that he had all the male children in the kingdom less than two years old killed.

Always have a good Hook or Headline whether you are selling in writing, verbally, or in a simple add.

A Hook or Headline can be equated to live bait.

AVisualHook

A visual hook can be equated to a fishing lure. It attracts the "buyers" attention through visual means.

In the case of Jesus Christ, think of the Cross. Everybody knows what the cross represents.

If you see a cross in front of a church, it is a

Christian Church. Some people use the cross

as inspiration. For example, they

imagine the cross with Jesus nailed to it.

No matter what happens in your day, no matter how many times you are turned down and don't make the sell, no matter how many sacrifices you have made, this doesn't compare to being nailed to a cross with a crown of thorns placed on your head.

Use visual hooks to sell; this may be in the form of a logo, a photo of your product, or an actually showing of your product to a potential buyer.

You can also use visual hooks to inspire yourself. For example, you may think to yourself what Napoleon do if he was a salesman?

Would he give up easily? Would he keep going and move on to other potential customers? Would he eventually succeed?

What does Napoleon have to do with Jesus Christ? You might be surprised to know that Napoleon used the story and life of Jesus Christ as inspiration to keep going in spite of extreme difficulties and seemingly insurmountable odds.

Study

Jesus was constantly reading and studying the Old Testament/Scriptures (not called the Old Testament at the time).

Jesus was without a doubt, the greatest salesperson that ever existed and he didn't leave things to chance. He studied. He knew his product well.

Since not everyone is born a great sales person, we can study. We must study not only our products and services, but also how to sell them.

In order to be able to really sell we must know

every aspect of sales. Also, if you will study

everything you can read, hear, or watch about
copywriting and direct marketing, you will
become a much greater
salesperson.

StoryTelling

Jesus Christ was always telling stories or parables. Each story led the listener closer to the desired outcome. Many of the stories contained lots of salt to keep the listener thirsty.

Ronald Regan and Bill Clinton had two different backgrounds. They had two different story lines. But both told magnificent stories and were able to work with both Democrats and Republicans by using stories to get their messages across.

This is a biggy. Learn to tell stories. As the old saying goes, "you have to tell to sell." This is still very true.

Salting

Salt is mentioned throughout the Bible. During this time salt had two purposes. First to give flavor to food. Secondly, to preserve food.

Likewise, this metaphorical salt gives flavor to stories and preserves the story by making the reader want to continue listening or reading what you have to say.

When Jesus told stories people listened. They wanted to know what he was going to say next. He did this by adding salt.

You can use salt by saying things like…."there are seven reasons for buying my product"…."in a few moments I will tell you three things that sets our product apart" etc.

These statements or questions keep the listener alert and waiting to hear or read what is coming next.

The greatest sales people know how to use salt well to keep prospects "thirsty" for more.

I personally learned about using the salting technique from reading the works of the great Gary Smalley and listening to him speak.

The next time you watch the News count how many times you hear something like…"coming up we will be discussing ….."

This is salt. Use it well, sparingly, but graciously.

WordPictures

Jesus used word pictures to create a visual understanding of what he was saying. Throughout his parables he used metaphors to compare the complex with the simple so that people could easily understand.

Word pictures are words that almost appear to leap off the page or out of your mouth. They describe what you want to say in such a way that a few words give meaning to what you want to say.

The great copywriter, Eugene Schwartz used word pictures better than anyone.

For example, he used the headline. "At Last –

Instant Beauty" These simple words written or

spoken together in the right order
create a word picture.

PowerWords

Jesus also used power words to give his message power and to make them more memorable.

Power words are words which give your sales pitch or written sales message power.

One of the power words used throughout the Bible is "fear. "Another power word is "love." Each of these words not only say something, they evoke a feeling inside of the reader.

In sales, "free" is still a great power word. Even though a "free sample" is almost expected now, it still works well.

Repetition

When talking one on one with a person or talking to large crowds, Jesus didn't only tell a story once then forget about it. He used repetition and retelling of stories so that people understood them and remembered them.

He also knew how to get to the same point by using different stories and keeping people interested.

GoodClosing

Jesus was a master at closing. Thousands of books have been written about how to close the sell.

Read the stories of Jesus and you are likely to understand how to truly close the sale.

Testimonials

Experts in Direct Marketing, Copywriting, and Advertising, like me sometimes forget that we didn't invent the use of testimonials. Jesus used testimonials from others to get his points across.

Value

What Jesus was offering had true value. In fact, he was offering a true value for free. It is little wonder why people still choose the value that he offered. Great value vs Little cost. It's practically a can't lose proposition.

Always offer more value than what your product or service is worth and you will have no problem selling it.

AFollowing

Long before the invention of the internet, FaceBook, Twitter, or LinkedIn, Jesus had a true following. People were interested to know what he was doing, saying, and what he would be doing next.

With social media if used correctly it is now easy to build our following.

WordOfMouth

The news of Jesus and his healing of the sick spread throughout the world. Again, he provided such value that almost everybody wanted what he had to offer.

People came from all parts to the world to see him, hear him speak, and watch him perform miracles? They are still talking about him today.

Humility

Jesus knew the value of being and showing humility when appropriate.

Don't forget to be humble when appropriate.

Boldness

Apart from being humble, Jesus was also bold. He took bold action and made bold statements even though he knew there would be consequences.

Use boldness to your advantage.

FreeSamples

We can think of Jesus healing the sick as giving away free samples. He showed what can happen with belief, faith, and trust.

Give away free samples when possible. But don't give away so much that there is no need to come back for more.

RagsToRiches

All the world loves a rags to riches or "poor boy does good" story. Jesus went from being a carpenter born in a manger to being a King. Is there a better rags to riches story?

ReluctantHero

The reluctant hero is someone who didn't necessarily choose to be put in a certain situation. But since they have been put in the situation, given the burden, or given the responsibility, they are going to give it their all.

It does not mean that the person is forced to do something. It simply means they were reluctant at first.

This technique works really well in sales.

Community

Jesus definitely knew how to build a community. People gathered around him to listen to him speak and perform miracles. The building of religious communities has continued for thousands of years.

Social media, email lists, websites, and blogs can be used to build your sales and consumer community.

Gifts

Jesus gave gifts without expecting anything in return. This is slightly different from giving away free samples. This builds good faith and trust.

Which charities could use your products or services?

Food

Jesus, like all great salesmen, gave away free food.

Keep bringing the donuts or bagels to your sales meetings when meeting with a group. And keep taking people to lunch. It works.

LimitedSupply

Jesus used the limited supply technique by reminding people that you don't know when you are going to die. There is a limited supply of time, so people have to make a choice before it is too late to accept the offer.

Limited supply techniques are an important part of any sales campaign and when used correctly can produce amazing results.

The key is to know what is limited. For example, Jesus didn't limit his love or forgiveness, but time was the limiting factor.

Secrecy

Jesus knew how to keep a secret and advised his followers to learn to do the same. The comment about "don't let your left hand know what your right hand is doing" wasn't talking about hands. It was obviously a metaphor for knowing how to keep secrets.

BuildingASalesTeam

Jesus assembled and trained a sales team very early. Of course, we know them as the twelve apostles.

Build, train, and use your sales team wisely.

OnGoingTraining

Jesus didn't just give one speech and end it at that. He, like any great salesperson, provided ongoing training to both his sales team and his audience.

Perseverance

Jesus didn't give up. He kept going no matter what happened to him or his followers.

Don't give up easily.

Passion

Jesus had a burning passion for his product. In fact, passion makes selling anything easier.

If you don't have passion for your product or service you probably will not do well selling it.

BonusesorSweetingThePot

Have you ever watched the commercials that say, "but wait, if you call right now we will add another ……. absolutely free"?

Jesus also knew how to sweeten the pot. He offered not only salvation, but ever-lasting life.

Honesty

Jesus offered a bargain, great value for a fair price. But above all he was honest. He didn't try to cheat people or make short-term gains.

Plan

Jesus talked about building on rock and not sand. This was a metaphor for not building without a plan.

My dad built several churches with his own hands. He cut down trees and brush to turn areas overgrown with weeds into houses of worship. And he always had a plan before starting.

Similarly, you should have a clear plan for your sales campaign. It can be adjusted and adapted as needed, but don't start without a written plan.

CauseandEnd(Reward)

If you don't remember anything from this short book remember this.

People will do some things for a cause. But they will not do them really well.

People will do some things for an end or reward. But they will not do them well.

But people will move mountains when they are motivated by both a cause and a reward.

Many battles have been fought over religion because there is both a cause and a reward in the minds of the warriors.

Find and share the cause and reward for yourself, your company, and your sales team.

In Closing:

I hope you have enjoyed this short book. Feel free to write me. I get lots of emails so I may not be able to answer all of them, but I will try to read each of them.

I have not included verses from the Bible in this first edition. I will endeavor to include them in the second edition.

Thanks,

Michael Von Irvin

Please recommend this book to three friends or contacts who may benefit from it. My other books can be found at amazon books by typing in "If Jesus Were A Salesman" and "Money Attraction".

Thank You.

(I have packed my Free Newsletters, chalk full of interesting information on business and wealth growth to help keep my subscribers current. You can only get this by signing up

Michael Irvin is an internationally recognized as health expert, marketing expert, businessman, and author who has helped others earn millions of dollars. He has helped people in just about every business category turn their ideas into fortunes. Michael's "The Little Guys Way To Riches" strategies are straight forward and he aims to cut through the hype found in typical business and health related world. His advice has been given and accepted by successful people throughout the world. He wrote the "The Little Guy's Way To Riches Series (www.nohogwashbooks.com) in order to give straight
forward information without the hype. For more money making and marketing tips and techniques, tactics, and strategies, go to

www.ingramcontent.com/pod-product-compliance
Lightning Source LLC
Chambersburg PA
CBHW030521220526
45463CB00007B/2666